# Saints & Seasons

## A Guide to New Mexico's Most Popular Saints

### By Ana Pacheco

Art by Marie Romero Cash.

# About the Covers

**Front Cover: Los Protectores**
This piece includes saints who are recognized as protectors of home and family. Because Marian images are a favorite of mine, I chose three representations. The number three (signifying the Trinity) also plays an important role in the imagery and theme of this piece.

*Top row, left to right:* San Gabriel Arcángel, protector of small children; San Miguel Arcángel, patron against all evil, guardian of children; San Rafael Arcángel, patron of travelers, marriage and good health, against blindness.

*Middle row, left to right:* Nuestra Señora de San Juan de Los Lagos, Nuestra Señora de Guadalupe, Nuestra Señora de la Purísima Concepción. Mary is known for help in distress and danger and is patroness against all evil, for compassion and healing.

*Bottom row, left to right:* San Francisco de Asís, patron of small animals and birds, reconciliation within the family, for peace; San José Patriarca, patron of fathers, carpenters, builders, the home, laborers, families and a happy death; San Lorenzo, protector against fire, patron of the poor, of cooks.

**Back Cover: Las Mujeres Santas**
The imagery in this piece came as a result of my desire to honor Our Lady of Guadalupe and women saints. Santa Teresita and Santa Rita were among my mother's favorites, and after her death in 2003, it became important to include saints she especially loved.

*Top row, left to right:* Santa Gertrudis, patroness of students and educators; Santa Librada, patroness of independent and liberated women; Santa Rita de Casia, patroness of marriage and keeping husbands faithful, of desperate causes, infertility and parenthood.

*Bottom row, left to right:* Santa Bárbara, patroness of the home, against lightning and fire, of architects, builders, and firemen; Nuestra Señora de Guadalupe, for favors in sickness, against all evil, war, for healing and motherly comfort; Santa Teresita de Lisieux, for aircraft pilots, aviators, bodily ills, florists, flower growers, against illness, loss of parents, missionaries, parish missions.

All traditional materials and techniques have been incorporated into my *retablos*. Often the pine panels are carved, and homemade gesso (a combination of animal-hide glue and gypsum) has been applied. The pigments used are produced from natural materials: Yellows and oranges are from iron oxides; blue is from indigo; reds and magentas are from cochineal (a small beetle picked off cactus plants); black walnut and micaceous clay are used for shades of brown. The finished *retablo* is sealed with a *piñón*-sap varnish. I also incorporate 23K gold leaf accents.    **—Arlene Cisneros Sena**

**Inside Front Cover: La Conquistadora**
La Conquistadora was first brought to New Mexico by Fray Alonso de Benavides in 1625. At that time he referred to the statue as Tránsito de la Virgen. After the Pueblo Revolt, Diego de Vargas returned the statue to Santa Fe and she was called La Conquistadora. Three hundred years after the 1692–1693 recolonization of New Mexico, she was called Our Lady of Peace, or Nuestra Señora de la Paz, by retired Archbishop Roberto Sánchez. This blue-on-white *retablo* style was influenced by Chinese blue-on-white ceramics, Spanish Majolica and Puebla blue-on-white ceramics from colonial Mexico. Blue-on-white ceramics were copied around the world in the 16th, 17th, 18th and 19th centuries. Additionally, the color blue is the color of protection, and also the color associated with the *manta* of the Blessed Virgin Mary. The color blue that is used over doors and windows in New Mexico was introduced by the early Spanish settlers, who brought this style from Moorish Spain.
**—Charles M. Carrillo**

**Inside Back Cover: Jesucristo**
The image of Jesus Christ being crucified is shown in detail in this sterling-silver reliquary with a glazed mica finish. Natural pigments of indigo, black walnut and yellow ochre were use to create this piece. This work of art, which was created in the 1980s, is very special to me because Jesus is still alive.
**—Ramón José López**

Dedicated to the memory of Pedro Ribera-Ortega

*El Mayordomo de La Conquistadora*

Heavenly Father, you are all holy and you call us to follow you faithfully. We thank you for the Saints presented in this book. They are our friends, already in heaven, who pray for us. They went before us and led holy and heroic lives of Christian faith. Help us to follow their example. Bless this book and all who read it with reverence and faith. We ask this through Christ Our Lord. Amen.

—*Archbishop Michael J. Sheehan*

Art by Ramón José López.

# Saints & Seasons

## A Guide to New Mexico's Most Popular Saints

### by Ana Pacheco

A *La Herencia* Publication

**Editor**
Nancy Zimmerman

**Associate Editors**
Walter K. López
Ree Strange Sheck

**Art Director**
Patrice Nightingale

**Photographer**
Linda Carfagno

*Saints & Seasons* was blessed by Archbishop Michael J. Sheehan
on September 23, 2005 at the Archdiocese Center of Santa Fe.

Copyright 2005, Gran Via Incorporated

FIRST EDITION

ISBN 0974302260
Library of Congress Control Number: 2005923522

Gran Via Incorporated
PO Box 22576
Santa Fe, NM 87502
www.herencia.com

**Santo Niño de Praga**

Art by Nicolás Otero.

# Acknowledgements

In reviewing *Saints & Seasons: A Guide to New Mexico's Most Popular Saints*, you'll quickly learn that this book is not a scholarly work, nor was it ever intended to be. The purpose of this book is to remind us of the importance that the saints, and the Roman Catholic calendar, have had in New Mexico for more than four hundred years. Throughout the state many parishes and mission churches honor saints as their patrons. Hopefully, this book filled with art, from the classical to the whimsical, created by some of New Mexico's most prolific contemporary *santeros*, will generate interest in learning more about the fascinating lives of the more than 3,000 saints that people from all over the world pray to each day. Not all of the New Mexico's popular saints are featured in this book, since a few of them have yet to be depicted by artists.

For your own personal library I highly recommend the following meticulously researched books that I used in putting this guide together: *Butler's Lives of the Saints*, *The Dictionary of Saints* by John J. Delaney, *Santos and Saints, The Religious Folk Art of Hispanic New Mexico* by Father Thomas J. Steele, *La Conquistadora, The Autobiography of an Ancient Statue* by Fray Angélico Chávez, *The New Mexico Santero* by E. Boyd, *Saints of the Pueblos* by Charles M. Carrillo, *Mexican Folk Retablos* by Gloria Fraser Giffords and my all-time favorite saint book, *Saints Preserve Us!* by Sean Kelly and Rosemary Rogers.

I'd like to express my sincere gratitude to the following people who helped to make this book possible: Bud Redding at the Spanish Colonial Arts Museum for steering me toward the incredibly talented artists whose work is featured in this book: to Marina Ochoa of the St. Francis Cathedral Archives, who graciously shared of the archive's records; to the Archdiocese of Santa Fe for prayers and encouragement in completing this project; to my cousin, Brother Steve Armenta, for his insight into the *santos* of New Mexico.

To Connie Hernández of the Old Santa Fe Trail Religious Shop for adding her endearing anecdotes in this book of a time long gone; to Dr. Jacqueline Orsini, the Marian scholar, for helping me understand the symbolism of each saint; to Kathy and Tessa Córdova for coming to my rescue—again! I'm especially grateful to the artists who selflessly gave of their time and more importantly, shared in their devotion.

# Table of Contents of the Saints

**St. Teresa de Liseux**

Art by Nicholás Otero.

# FROM THE AUTHOR

The world wasn't perfect for my mother's generation, the one that came of age during World War II, but people back then were fortunate to have what is lacking for many of us today: the belief that no matter what, their faith in God would get them through the most difficult times. Long before the days of antidepressants people sought help through prayer, and it was the saints who would intercede on their behalf. This form of communication with God gave people a sense of empowerment.

St. Teresa de Lisieux, the one referred to as the Little Flower, was my mother's favorite saint. She communicated with her through the mail. With regularity, some type of flower, usually a rose, made its way onto a card, letter, or Montgomery Ward catalog—St. Teresa was letting my mom know that her prayers had been heard

My mother kept an arsenal of saints in the house: The Virgin Mary, St. Teresa, San Martín de Porres, San Pelegrino, St. Dymphna, St. Lazarus, Jesus Christ, the Holy Family and crucifixes in every room. To ensure that we always had protection she moved the saints to different parts of the house. She also bathed the saints to keep them free from dust. Trouble was that all the attention my mother lavished on the saints began to wear them down. Several of the ceramic statues were chipped and a few had had their heads broken from being moved around so much. My mom would glue their heads back on but after a while they just fell off. Eventually, she just left their heads next to their bodies and that's how she prayed to them, headless and all.

The saints played an integral part in the lives of my extended family as well. I remember listening to my aunts and uncles talk about the saints when we'd visit on Sunday afternoons. They all had their favorites and they knew everything there was to know about them, just the way people keep abreast of a popular actor or sports hero today. Like my mother and her personal arrangement with the U.S. mail, they also had their own form of Morse code with the saints. Each week we received a progress report on the various ways the saints had let them know that their prayers had been heard.

Since the saints took such good care of my family, my family did its best to shower them with love and devotion. The Infant of Prague was the favorite saint of my *madrina*, Adelina Ortiz. Adelina and her sisters, Emilia and Lucinda, made the saint a complete wardrobe of velvet and satin. At the beginning of each new season they would change the Infant of Prague's outfit accordingly. In the spring and summer it consisted of mostly satin fabric in warm, cheerful hues, while in the colder months he wore a dark velvet robe. The Infant of Prague was the first one to greet us, as he stood majestically at his altar in the vestibule of the house when we'd visit the Ortiz sisters.

According to family lore, Our Lady of Guadalupe caused a schism on the Pacheco side of my family that lasted for several years. My Aunt Julia "Mana" Pacheco Martínez, being the eldest of eleven brothers and sisters, felt a matriarchal right to her mother's statue of Our Lady of Guadalupe when she died. But my grandmother, Juanita Pino Pacheco, had bequeathed the saint to one of her other daughters, Ruth "Fufo" Pacheco Armenta. This rift over the statue kept the two sisters from speaking to each other for a long time. It took some intercession from God, but the sisters eventually reconciled. Today, Our Lady of Guadalupe is in the home of Fufo's daughter, Lydia Armenta Rivera. Like any important family heirloom, the saints were passed down from generation to generation.

The *compadrazgo* system involving the baptizing of saints was similar to the christening of a child back in the old days. If anything happened to the people who owned the saint, the godparents became responsible for its care and veneration. The lives of my parents, Natalie Ortiz and Jesús Pacheco, were forever entwined with Pedro Ribera Ortega, to whom this book has been dedicated, when they became *padrinos* to his Santo Niño de Atocha.

Those of my parent's generation lived their lives through the saints and they knew that as long as they had faith there would always be hope.

—*Ana Pacheco*

**Flight from Egypt**

Art by Gabriel Vigil.

# January

**San Basilio (329–79)**
**Feast Day January 2**
Patron of Russia and hospital administrators and born in Caesarea, Cappadocia, Turkey. San Basilio was a learned man of great personal holiness, and one of the great orators of Christianity. He is a Doctor of the Church.
Art by Carlos Otero.

ST. ELIZABETH ANN SETON

**St. Elizabeth Ann Seton** (1774–1821)
**Feast Day January 4**

The founder of the American congregation of the Sisters of Charity, who established St. Vincent Hospital and Orphanage in the 19th century.
Art by Rubén Montoya.

**Epiphany**
**Feast Day January 6**

The twelve days of Christmas end with the Feast of Epiphany, also called The Adoration of the Magi or The Manifestation of God. Celebrated on January 6, it is known as the Day of the Three Kings. While the Western Christian church celebrates December 25th, the Eastern Christian Church to this day recognizes January 6 as the celebration of the nativity. January 6 is also recognized as Christ's physical birthday in Bethlehem.

Art by Arlene Cisneros Sena.

**San Sebastián (d. circa 288)**
**Feast Day January 20**

Patron of archers, athletes, doctors, hardware, pin makers, police and soldiers; invoked against plague. San Sebastián was born in Narbonne, Gaul, Italy, and in 283 became a soldier in the Roman army, where he made numerous converts to Christianity. When it was discovered that he was recruiting religious converts he was shot with arrows and martyred.

Art by Henry Parra.

**San Vicente de Zaragosa (d. 304)**
**Feast Day January 22**

Patron of charitable societies, hospital workers, prisoners and vintners, San Vicente was born at Huesca, Spain. He was tortured and died in prison when he refused to surrender the sacred books of the church. His relics continue to be venerated in Valencia, Spain.

Art by Carlos Otero.

**San Ildefonso (607–67)**
**Feast Day January 23**
Born in Toledo, Spain, where he was named archbishop in 657, San Ildefonso has been honored as a Doctor of the Spanish Church. Patron of San Ildefonso Pueblo, 25 miles north of Santa Fe.
Art by Charles M. Carrillo.

**San Francisco de Salas (1567-1622)**
**Feast Day January 24**

Patron of editors, journalists and writers; invoked against deafness. Born in the family castle at Thorens, Savoy, in France, San Francisco de Sales founded schools and made converts to Catholicism, as well as bringing many lapsed Catholics into the fold. Along with Frances de Chantal, he founded the Order of Visitation (the Visitandines). His writings have become spiritual classics and are widely read today. He was declared a Doctor of the Church in 1877 and designated the patron saint of the Catholic press in 1923.

Art by Nicolás Otero.

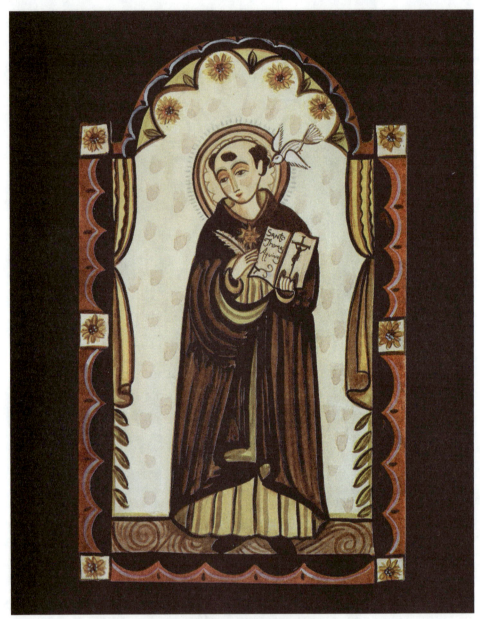

**Santo Tomás Aquinas (c.1225–74)**
**Feast Day January 28**

Patron of scholars, theologians and pencil makers, Santo Tomás Aquinas was born near Aquino, Italy, and joined the Dominican order in 1224. He is considered the greatest theological master of Christianity and his teachings have become the basis of modern Catholic theology. While stressing the distinction between faith and reason, he emphasized the existence of God by natural reason. Because of his intellectual prowess, Santo Tomás Aquinas is one of the most revered saints in the Catholic Church.

Art by Nicolás Otero.

# February

**Santa Brígida (c. 450–525)**
**Feast Day February 1**

Patroness of milkmaids, fugitives, newborns and nuns, Santa Brígida was born near Louth, Ireland. Her parents were baptized by St. Patrick and St. Brígida developed a close friendship with him. Both she and St. Patrick are the patron saints of Ireland. Around 470 she founded a monastery at Kildare where she became the abbess of the convent, the first in Ireland.

Art by Carlos Santistevan.

**San Felipe de Jesús (1571–97)**
**Feast Day February 6**

Patron of Mexico and youth, San Felipe de Jesús was born in Mexico City to Spanish parents. He became a Franciscan, then left the order to work as a merchant, a decision that he regretted. While on business in the Philippines he rejoined the Franciscans. On a trip back to Mexico to be ordained, his ship was driven off course to Japan, where he was crucified along with twenty-five other Christians in Nagasaki.

Art by Carlos Santistevan.

**San Valentín (d. circa 308)**
**Feast Day February 14**

Patron of lovers; the martyrdoms of three different saints named Valentine are celebrated on this day. One of these was a priest and physician who was beheaded in 269 on February 14. The custom of sending valentines stems from the belief that birds began to pair on that day.

Art by Polly E. Chávez.

# March

**San Albino (d. circa 550)**
**Feast Day March 1**

Patron of the sick, the indigent, widows and orphans. San Albino's feast day on March 1 was the very day long ago that the *acequia madre* in the town of Mesilla, N.M., was opened and the church was named for San Albino.
Art by Henry Parra.

**San Patricio (c. 389–461)**
**Feast Day March 17**

Patron of Ireland; invoked against snakes. St. Patrick converted Ireland to Christianity in 432. St. Patrick, who started out as a sheepherder, spent his life recruiting converts and was responsible for bringing Ireland into closer relations with the Western church. His is one of the most widely celebrated feast days in the world.

Art by Jean Anaya Moya.

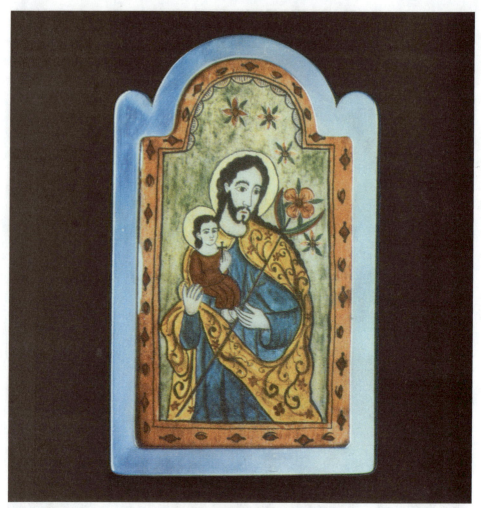

**San José (1st Century)**
**Feast Day March 19**

Patron of carpenters, fathers, happy death, house-hunting and laborers; invoked against communism and doubt. According to legend, the flowering staff of San José signifies God's choice for Mary's hand in marriage. St. Teresa and St. Francis de Sales helped spread the devotion of St. Joseph. San José is the patron saint of Laguna Pueblo in New Mexico

**Parish churches:** Our Lady of Sorrows, Bernalillo; St. Gertrude the Great, Mora; St. Rose of Lima, Santa Rosa; Our Lady of Sorrows, La Joya; St. Francis Xavier, Clayton; Sacred Heart of Jesús, Española; San Isidro/San José, Santa Fe; San Felipe de Neri, Albuquerque; San Miguel, Socorro; St. Anthony, Dixon; St. Mary, Vaughn; San Miguel del Vado, Ribera; Our Lady Of Guadalupe, Clovis; Holy Family, Chimayó; Our Lady of Sorrows, Las Vegas; Immaculate Heart of Mary, White Rock, N.M.

**Mission locations:** Algodones, Cañoncito, Colonias, Contreras, Folsom, Hernández, La Ciénega, Ledoux, Luis López, Lyden, Pinos Wells, San José, Texico, Trampas, Upper Rociada, N.M.

Art by Ramón José López.

**Gabriel the Archangel**
**Feast Day March 24**

Patron of childbirth, diplomats, messengers, postal workers, stamp collectors, telephone and television workers. San Gabriel, known as the angel of the annunciation, proclaimed the birth of Christ to Mary and foretold the birth of St. John the Baptist.

Art by Marie Sena.

# Primavera
# Easter

Moveable Feast

**The Last Supper**

Christians celebrate Easter on the Sunday after the first full moon following the Spring equinox. Easter is preceded by Lent, which is marked by a forty-weekday period of fasting and penitence starting with Ash Wednesday and ending at the close of Holy Week.

Art by Marie Sena.

**First Station: Jesus is condemned to death.**
Art by Marie Romero Cash courtesy of the Archdiocese of Santa Fe.

**Second Station: Jesus carries his Cross.**
Art by Marie Romero Cash courtesy of the Archdiocese of Santa Fe.

**Third Station: Jesus falls for the first time.**
Art by Marie Romero Cash courtesy of the Archdiocese of Santa Fe.

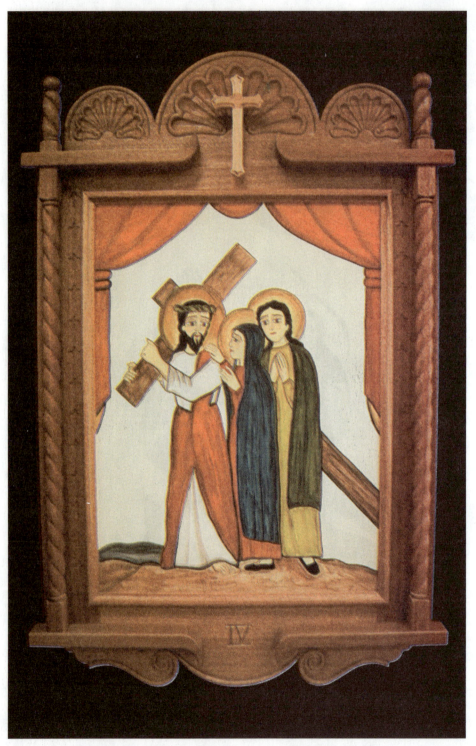

**Fourth Station: Jesus meets his afflicted mother.**
Art by Marie Romero Cash courtesy of the Archdiocese of Santa Fe.

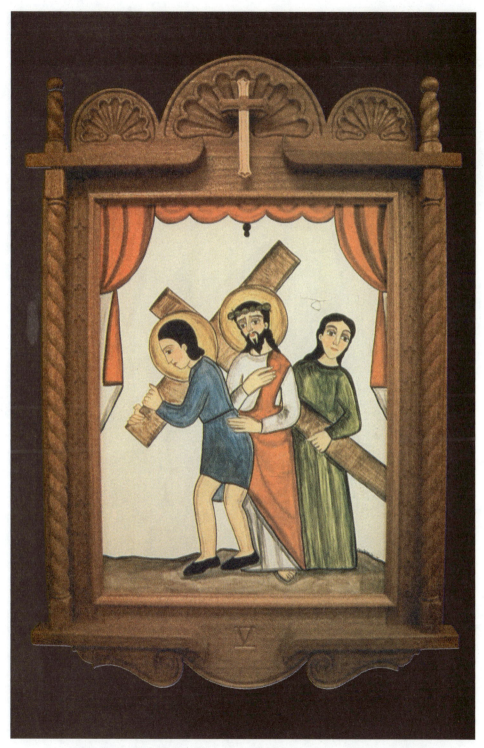

**Fifth Station: Simon of Cyrene helps Jesus carry his cross.**
Art by Marie Romero Cash courtesy of the Archdiocese of Santa Fe.

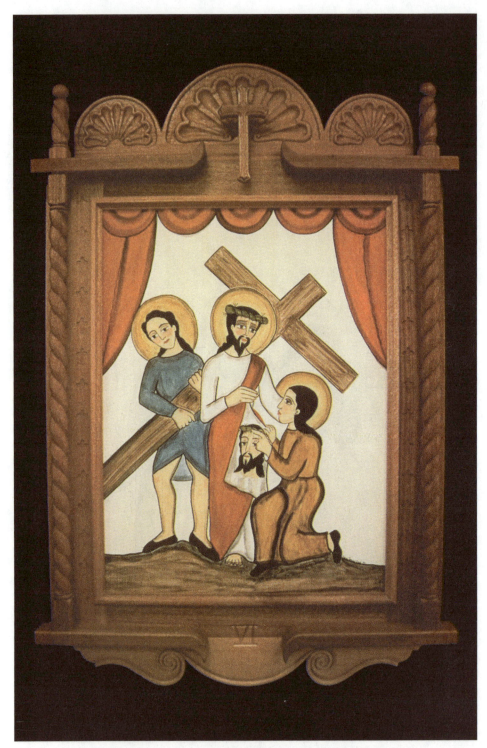

**Sixth Station: Verónica wipes the face of Jesus.**
Art by Marie Romero Cash courtesy of the Archdiocese of Santa Fe.

**Seventh Station: Jesus falls the second time.**
Art by Marie Romero Cash courtesy of the Archdiocese of Santa Fe.

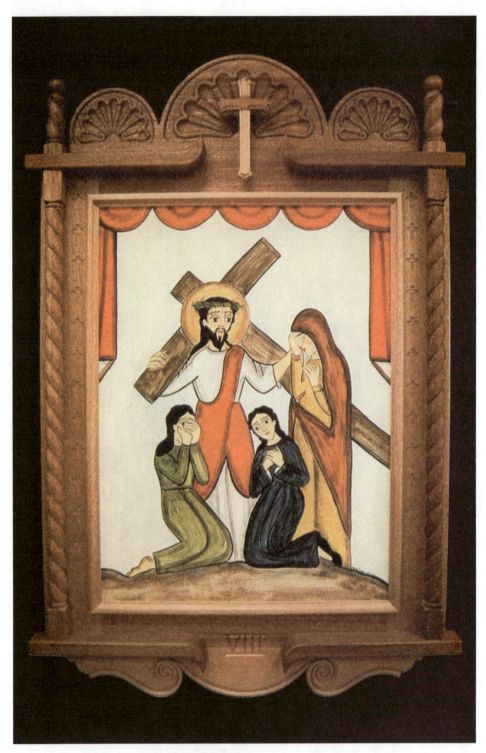

**Eighth Station: Jesus meets the women of Jerusalem.**
Art by Marie Romero Cash courtesy of the Archdiocese of Santa Fe.

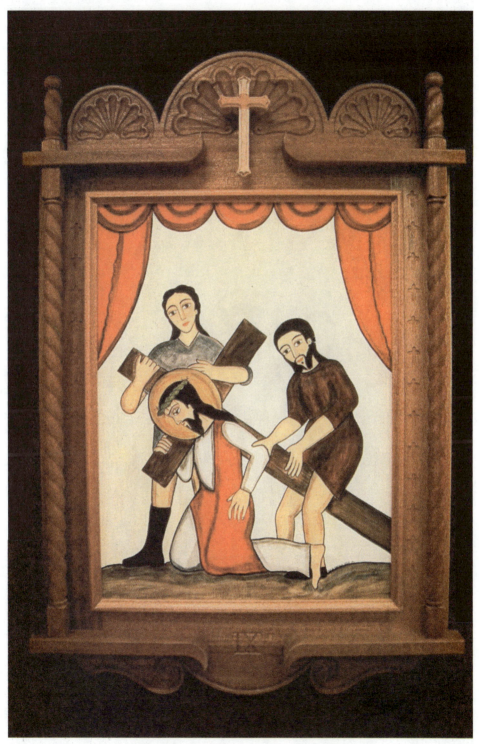

**Ninth Station: Jesus falls a third time.**
Art by Marie Romero Cash courtesy of the Archdiocese of Santa Fe.

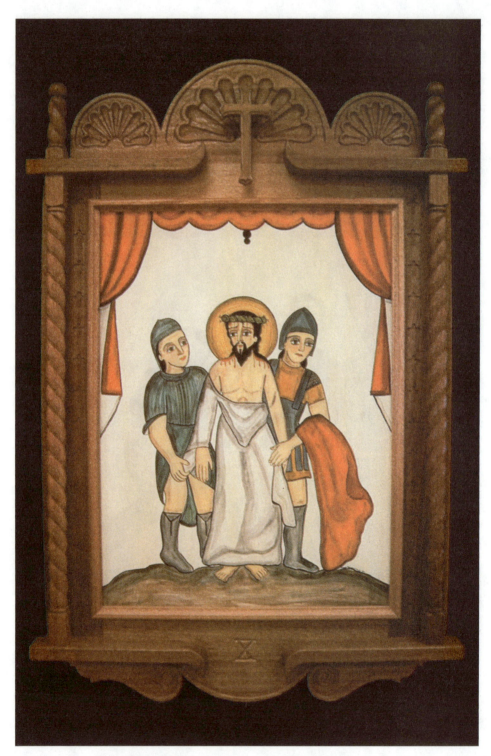

**Tenth Station: Jesus is stripped of his clothes.**
Art by Marie Romero Cash courtesy of the Archdiocese of Santa Fe.

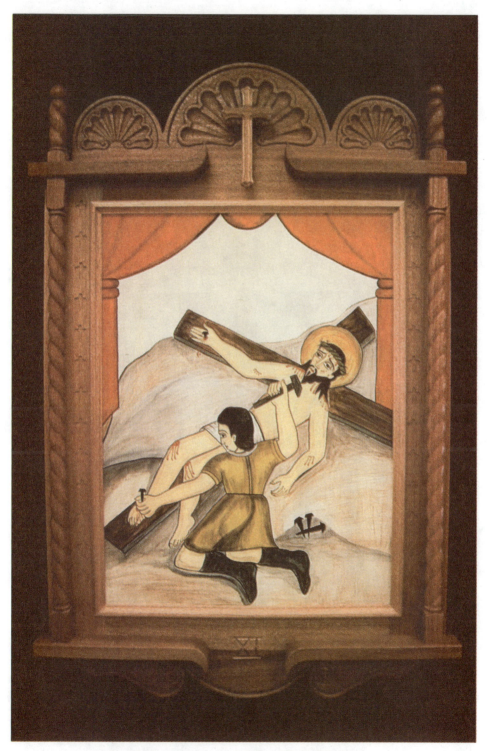

**Eleventh Station: Jesus is nailed to the cross.**
Art by Marie Romero Cash courtesy of the Archdiocese of Santa Fe.

**Twelfth Station: Jesus dies on the cross.**
Art by Marie Romero Cash courtesy of the Archdiocese of Santa Fe.

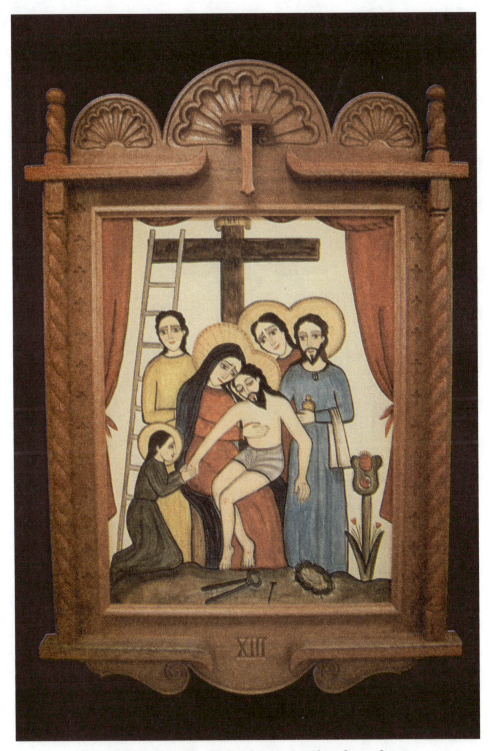

**Thirteenth Station: The body of Jesus is taken from the cross.**
Art by Marie Romero Cash courtesy of the Archdiocese of Santa Fe.

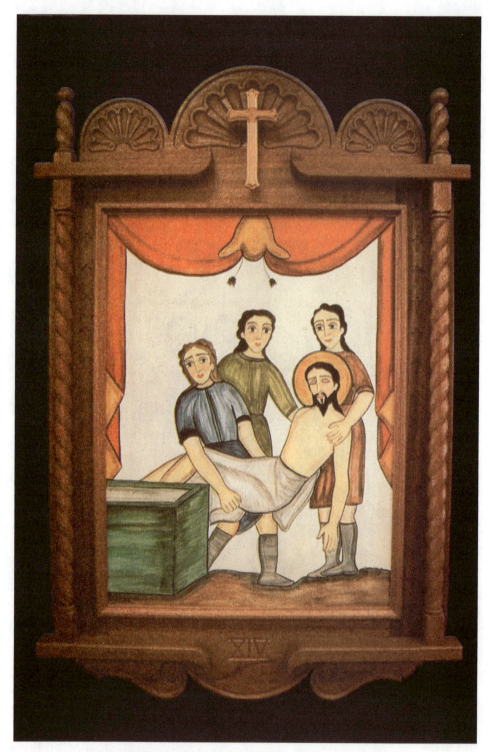

**Fourteenth Station: Jesus is laid in the tomb.**
Art by Marie Romero Cash courtesy of the Archdiocese of Santa Fe.

Easter

**St. John-Baptist de la Salle (1651–1719)**
**Feast Day April 7**
Patron of schoolteachers and founder of Los Hermanos de las Escuelas Cristianas.
The Christian brothers have been in Santa Fe since 1859, when they founded
St. Michael's High School and the College of Santa Fe.
Art by Nicolás Otero.

### St. Bernadette (1844–79)
### Feast Day April 16

Patroness of shepherds, Bernadette was born in Lourdes, France, on January 7.
The Mother of God appeared to Bernadette in this southwestern part of France in
1858. Bernadette's story became internationally known through the popular
movie, *The Song of Bernadette*.

Art by Arthur López.

**St. George (d. circa 303)**
**Feast Day April 23**

Patron saint of horses, equestrians, farmers, Boy Scouts, knights, archers and armorers; invoked against the plague, leprosy and syphilis. The mythological slayer of dragons, St. George was considered a hero among the Crusaders during the Middle Ages.

Art by Gabriel Vigil.

**St. Zita (128–78)**
**Feast Day April 27**

Patroness of housemaids and domestic servants; invoked in the search for lost keys. Born in Monte Sagrati, Italy, St. Zita was a servant for forty-eight years. She also worked to alleviate the suffering of the poor and criminals in prison.
Art by Gustavo Victor Goler.

# Mes de María

Dedicated to the Virgin Mary with the crowning of Our Lady on Mother's Day.

**Nuestra Señora de Alma**

Art by Gabriel Vigil.

**Nuestra Señora del Camino**

Art by Ramón José López.

**Nuestra Señora de la Luz**

Art by Gustavo Victor Goler.

**Nuestra Señora de San Juan de los Lagos**

Art by Frankie Lucero.

May

**Nuestra Señora de Merced**

Art by Arturo Olivas.

**Nuestra Señora Purísima**

Art by Marie Sena.

**Nuestra Señora de Valencia**

Art by Monica Sosaya Halford.

# May

**St. Joseph (1st Century)**
**Feast Day May 1**

St. Joseph, whose feast day is March 19, is also venerated on May Day throughout the world as the patron of all workers. On this day in New Mexico it is also customary to plant hollyhocks (*varas de San José*) outside the kitchen door.
Art by Carlos Otero.

**San Peregrino (1260–1345)**
**Feast Day May 1**

Patron saint for those suffering from cancer, Laziosi Peregrine was born in Forli, Italy, to a wealthy family. Suffering from cancer of the foot, San Peregrino was to have his foot amputated when Jesus Christ climbed down from the crucifix on the wall and cured him completely. He was canonized in 1726.

Art by Horacio Córdova.

**St. Florián (d. 304)**
**Feast Day May 4**

Patron of brewers, chimney sweeps and firefighters; invoked against drowning, fire and floods. An officer of the Roman army, St. Florián was drowned in the year 304 for professing his Christianity.

Art by Jean Anaya Moya.

### St. Dymphna (d. circa 650)
### Feast Day May 15

Patroness of asylums and mental-health workers; invoked against epilepsy, insanity and sleepwalking. St. Dymphna was killed by her father in the seventh century when she refused his sexual advances. Today, some 1,300 years later, the connection between mental illness and sexual abuse in children is considered an established fact.

Art by Arlene Cisneros Sena.

### San Isidro (1070–1130)
### Feast Day May 15

Patron of farmers, farm workers and ranchers, San Isidro was born near Madrid, Spain, in the 11th century. In New Mexico he is prayed to for rain and a bountiful harvest. Patron of the abandoned Gran Quivira Pueblo in New Mexico.

**Parish churches:** Holy Family, Roy; St. Joseph, Mosquero; St. Rose of Lima, Santa Rosa; Holy Child, Tijeras; Nuestra Señora de Guadalupe, Villanueva; Holy Cross, Santa Cruz; Our Lady of Sorrows, La Joya; San Francisco de Asís, Ranchos de Taos; St. Gertrude the Great, Mora; Holy Family, Chimayó; San Miguel del Vado, Ribera; San Diego Mission, Jemez Pueblo; St. Joseph, Springer; Our Lady of Sorrows, N.M.

**Mission locations:** Albert, Borica, Escobosa, Gonzales Ranch, La Mesilla, Las Nutrias, Las Córdovas/Cordillera, Ojo Feliz, Río Chiquito, San Isidro Norte, San Isidro Sur, San Ysidro, Sedillo, Tinaja, Trujillo, N.M.

Art by Marie Sena.

**San Juan Nepomuceno (c. 1340–93)**
**Feast Day May 16**

Patron of bridges, bridge builders, Bohemia and confessors; invoked against slander; born at Nepomuk, Bohemia. The veneration of this saint came to New Mexico with the Third Order of St. Francis, from which came the Brotherhood of the Penitentes.

**Parish churches:** St. Patrick, Chama; Holy Child, Tijeras; San Antonio de Padua, Peñasco; San Miguel del Vado, Ribera, N.M.

**Mission locations:** Canjilón, Chililí, Llano de San Juan, San Juan, N.M.

Art by Ramón José López.

**San Pascual**
**Feast Day May 17**
Patron of shepherds, cooks and the kitchen; invoked against sad spirits. San
Pascual came from Aragón, Spain, in the 1540s where he joined the Franciscans.
San Pascual's image can be found in most New Mexico kitchens.
Art by Arlene Cisneros Sena.

**Our Lady of Light**
**Feast Day May 21**

Our Lady of Light is commonly prayed to by soldiers requesting guidance as they prepare for battle.

**Parish church:** St. Anthony of Padua, Pecos, N.M.

**Mission lcoation:** Cañoncito, N.M.

Art by Jean Anaya Moya.

**Santa Rita (1381–1457)**
**Feast Day May 22**

Patroness of desperate causes, abused women; invoked against bleeding, infertility, loneliness, tumors, unhappy marriage and spousal infidelity. Santa Rita, who was born near Spoleto, Italy, was married against her will at the age of 12 to a local gangster in Italy, who abused her. After he was murdered, both of her sons died and she fulfilled her lifelong dream of becoming a nun.

**Parish churches:** San Miguel del Vado, Ribera; San Miguel, Socorro; St. Gertrude the Great, Mora, N.M.

**Mission locations:** Bernal, Lucero, Riley, N.M.

Art by Henry Parra.

**San Bernardo (c. 996–1081)**
**Feast Day May 28**

Patron of skiers and mountain climbers, St. Bernard of Montjoux spent more than four decades doing missionary work in the Alps. Two mountain tops in the Alps and the St. Bernard dog are named after him.

Art by Gustavo Victor Goler.

**Corpus Christi**
**Moveable Feast Day**

The year 2005 was proclaimed the Year of the Eucharist with Corpus Christi falling on May 29. The celebration of Corpus Christi has a long history in New Mexico, where processions of the Holy Eucharist were regularly held in the streets with incense, prayer, hymns and the benediction of the Blessed Sacrament at various altars. Corpus Christi is the first of three special Sundays in the spring followed by the Roman Catholic calendar.

Art by Charles M. Carrillo.

**Joan of Arc (1412–31)**
**Feast Day May 30**

Patroness of France and the military, Joan of Arc was canonized in 1920. Born at Domrémy, France, Joan of Arc's notoriety as a soldier has become synonymous with that of triumph and courage. Thought to be a witch by the English, she was burned at the stake on May 30, 1431.

**Parish church:** St. Anne, Tucumcari, N.M.

**Mission location:** Montoya, N.M.

Art by Frankie Lucero

**Sagrado Corazón**
**Moveable Feast, Celebrated the Friday after Corpus Christi**
On this day it's customary to pray to soften the hearts of mean people.
**Parish churches:** Holy Family, Roy; St. Joseph, Mosquero; St. Anthony, Questa and San José; St. Xavier, Clayton; Nuestra Señora de Guadalupe, Pojoaque; St. Anne, Tucumcari; St. Gertrude the Great, Mora; Holy Family, Chimayó; Santa Clara, Wagon Mound, N.M.
**Mission locations:** Bueyeros, Costilla, Dilia, Moses, Nambé, Nara Visa, Rainsville, Río Chiquito, Watrous, N.M.
Art by Marie Sena.

# June

**Holy Trinity**
**Moveable Feast Day celebrated after Corpus Christi**
The Trinity signifies the central doctrine of Christian religion with unity of the Godhead. There are three persons: the Father, the Son and the Holy Spirit. The Father is God, the Son is God and the Holy Spirit is God, and yet there are not three Gods but one God.
**Parish church:** St. Francis Xavier, Clayton, N.M.
**Mission location:** Hayden, N.M.
Art by Arlene Cisneros Sena.

### San Antonio de Padua (1195–1231)
### Feast Day June 13

Patron saint of Portugal, the harvest, the poor, spinsters; invoked against infertility and those looking for lost objects. Born in Padua, Italy, St. Anthony started out in the Augustine Order but changed habits to become a Franciscan in 1219. Mothers pray to this saint to aid in their daughters' search for a good husband. Patron saint of Sandía Pueblo in New Mexico.

**Parish churches:** Our Lady of Sorrows, La Joya; St. Gertrude the Great, Mora; Nuestra Señora de Guadalupe, Pojoaque; San Juan Nepomuceno, El Rito; San José, Los Ojos; San Miguel, Holy Child, Tijeras; Estancia Valley, Moriarty, St. Alice, Mountainair; Immaculate Conception, Las Vegas; La Santísima Trinidad, Arroyo Seco, N.M.

**Mission locations:** Abeytas, Cedar Crest, Chacón, Cleveland, El Rancho, Placitas, Sabinal, San Antonio, Sevilleta, Tajique, Tapia, Torreón, Upper Town, Valdez, N.M.
Art by Arthur López.

# Verano

**San Luis Gonzaga (1568–91)**
**Feast Day June 21**

Patron of youth; St. Aloysius Gonzaga was born in Lombardy, France, and is considered a role model for the Jesuits and their students.

**Parish church:** San Juan Nepomuceno, El Rito, N.M.

**Mission location:** Las Tablas, N.M.

Art by Frankie Lucero.

**San Acacio (d. circa 303)**
**Feast Day June 22**

Patron invoked against headaches. A Cappadocian by birth, San Acadio was scourged and beheaded for his faith. One of the oldest churches in the San Luis Valley in southern Colorado is named for San Acacio.

**Parish churches:** St. Gertrude the Great, Mora; San Antonio de Padua, Peñasco, N.M.
**Mission locations:** Golondrinas and Llano Largo, N.M.
Art by Carlos Otero.

**Immaculate Heart of Mary**
**Feast Day June 23**
**Parish church:** St. Gertrude the Great, Mora, N.M.
**Mission location:** Holman, N.M.
Art by Arlene Cisneros Sena.

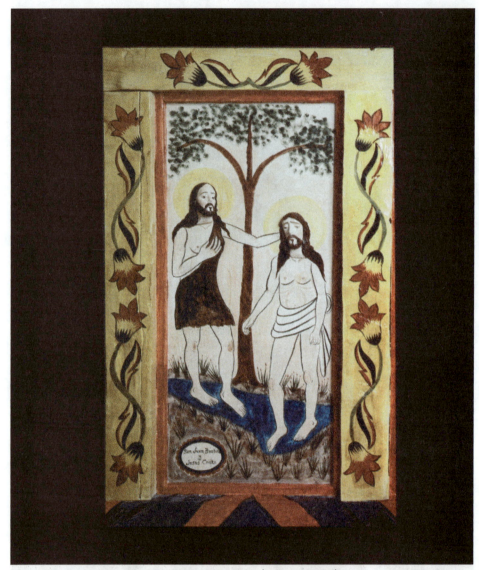

### San Juan Bautista (1st Century)
### Feast Day June 24

Patron of auto routes, candle makers, farriers, health spas, workers in leather, road and wool industries. La Fiesta de San Juan Bautista is the traditional day for *acequias* to be blessed so that the water can fructify the crops. Also during this celebration, the men of the villages in New Mexico used to perform La Corrida de los Gallos, in which the horseman would attempt to grab a buried rooster and run with it before getting caught by the rest of the players. Patron saint of San Juan Pueblo in New Mexico.

**Parish churches:** St. Thomas the Apostle, Abiquiú; St. Mary, Vaughn; San Miguel, Socorro; Santa Clara, Wagon Mound; Our Lady of Sorrows, La Joya, N.M.
**Mission locations:** Coyote, Durán, Kelly, Los le Febres, Veguita, N.M.
Art by Ramón José López.

**San Pedro (d. circa 64)**
**Feast Day June 29**

Patron of boat builders, clockmakers, fishermen and net makers; invoked against fever, foot trouble and wolves. Known as the gatekeeper of Heaven, St. Peter was one of the apostles and the brother of St. Andrew, also an apostle.

**Parish churches:** St. John the Baptist, San Juan Pueblo; Estancia Valley, Moriarty; Holy Cross, Santa Cruz; St. Thomas the Apostle, Abiquiú, N.M.

**Mission locations:** Chamita, Estancia, San Pedro; Youngsville, N.M.

Art by Monica Sosaya Halford.

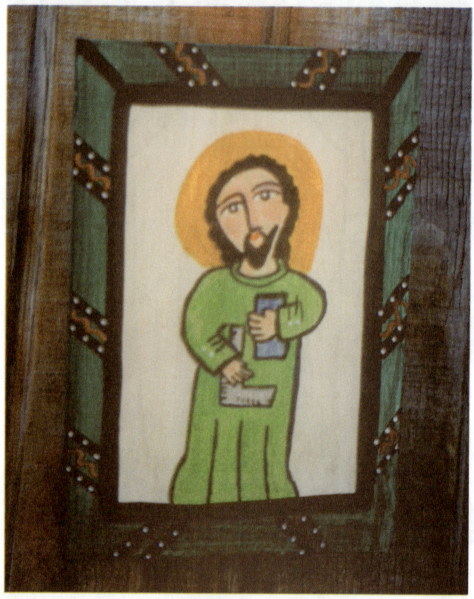

**Santo Tomás (1st Century)**
**Feast Day July 3**

Patron of architects, builders, construction workers, carpenters, geometricians, masons, and surveyors; invoked against blindness and doubt. One of the original apostles, born in Galilee, Santo Tomás was the twin brother of St. James, also an apostle. Santo Tomás brought the gospel to India, where he was martyred and buried near Madras. In 1972 Pope Paul VI declared him the apostle of India. Art by Richard Montoya.

**Our Lady of Refuge**
**Feast Day July 4**
**Parish church:** St. Rose of Lima, Santa Rosa, N.M.
**Mission location:** Puerto de Luna, N.M.
Art by Ramón José López.

**St. Benedict** (c. 480–547)
**Feast Day July 11**

Patron of architects, coppersmiths, the dying, farm workers, monks and servants; invoked against gallstones, poison and witchcraft. Born in Nursia, near Rome, St. Benedict became an expert in both scripture and sacred music at a very young age. He was the founder of Western monasticism; there is a monastery in Pecos, New Mexico, named after him. Pope Paul VI named St. Benedict the patron of Europe in 1964.

Art by Nicolás Otero.

**Santa Verónica (1st Century)**
**Feast Day July 12**

Patroness of laundresses, Santa Verónica is featured in the sixth station of the cross, where she wiped the blood and perspiration from Jesus Christ's brow with her handkerchief, leaving the imprint of his face on it. Bullfighters in Spain refer to the drawing of their cape across the bull's face as a *verónica*.
Art by Frankie Lucero.

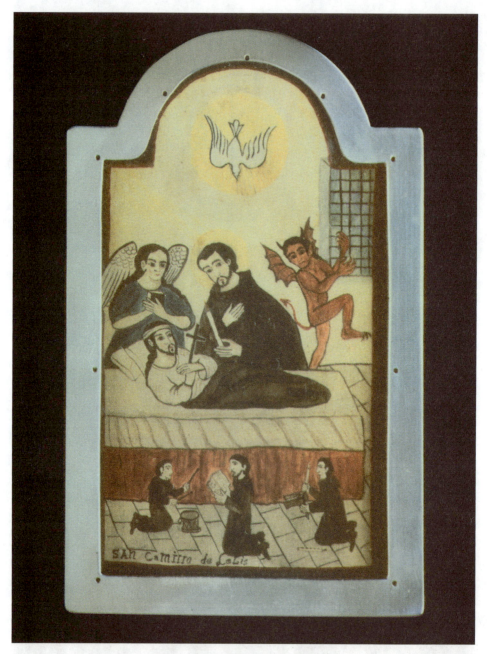

**San Camio de Lelis (1550–1614)**
**Feast Day July 14**

Patron of hospitals, nurses and the sick; invoked against gambling. San Camio de Lelis was born in Bocchianico, Itlay, and became a *penitente* after losing all of his worldly possessions through gambling. As a repentant, he worked as a nurse with San Felipe de Neri, founding the Servants of the Sick, a congregation of male nurses.

Art by Ramón José López.

**Blessed Kateri Tekakwitha (1656–80)**
**Feast Day July 14**

Known as the Lily of the Mohawks, St. Kateri Tekakwitha is the first Native American saint. The daughter of a Christian Algonquin who was captured by Iroquois Indians and married to a Mohawk, she was born at the Indian village of Osserneon in Auriesville, New York. She was beatified in 1980 by Pope John Paul II. Art by Krissa Maria López-Moya.

**Our Lady of Mt. Carmel**
**Feast Day July 16**

Patroness of the souls in purgatory. Our Lady of Carmel is known for her devotion to the scapular, which she gave us in the 12th century. Her scapular is a sign of consecration of María Santísima. The order of Carmelites came to Santa Fe in 1945.
**Parish churches:** Nativity of the Blessed Virgin Mary, Alameda; San Juan Nepomuceno, El Rito; St. Gertrude the Great, Mora; San Francisco de Asís, Ranchos de Taos; St. Joseph, Springer, N.M.
**Mission locations:** Alameda, Cañón Plaza, El Carmen, Llano Quemado, Palo Blanco, N.M.
Art by Monica Sosaya Halford.

### Santa Librada
**Feast Day July 20**

Patroness of liberated women; invoked against men. Also known as Wilgefortis, Liberata Kummernis in Germay, Uncumber in England, and Livrade in France, Santa Librada was one of nine daughters born to a pagan Portuguese king. He wanted her to marry King Wilgefortis of Sicily, but she resisted by growing a beard and mustache. Her father was so furious that he had her crucified. From the cross Santa Librada promised aid to those with cruel or difficult husbands. Art by Monica Sosaya Halford.

**Santa María Magdalena (1st Century)**
**Feast Day July 22**

Patroness of contemplatives, fallen women, glovers, hairdressers and perfumers, Mary Magdalene was the sister of St. Martha and St. Lazarus. Throughout history she has been maligned as a fallen women but was staunchly defended by Christ and was witness to his resurrection.

**Parish church:** San Miguel, Socorro, N.M.

**Mission location:** Magdalena, N.M.

Art by Arturo Olivas.

**San Cristóbal (d. circa 251)**
**Feast Day July 25**

Patron of bachelors, bus drivers, ferryboat pilots, horsemen, police officers, skiers, travelers, truck drivers; invoked against nightmares, peril from water, plague, sudden death and tempests. St. Christopher was a powerfully built man who wandered the world in search of novelty and adventure. He came upon a hermit who lived beside a dangerous stream and served others by guiding them to safe places to cross. He was martyred circa 251 and removed from sainthood by Rome in 1989. St. Christopher continues to have many followers.

**Parish church:** La Santísima Trinidad, Arroyo Seco, N.M.
**Mission location:** San Cristóbal, N.M.
Art by Jean Anaya Moya.

### Santiago de Compostela (1st Century)
### Feast Day July 25

Patron of Guatemala, Spain, Nicaragua, veterinarians, horsemen, laborers, furriers and soldiers; invoked against arthritis and rheumatism. El Santuario de Chimayó is dedicated to St. James, the apostolic martyr and first Christian teacher-apostle. Thought to be a cousin or twin brother of St. Thomas, St. James is known as the defender of Christianity in Spain against the Moors. His remains can be found in Compostela, Spain, to which thousands of pilgrimages are made annually.

**Parish churches:** Our Lady of Sorrows, Las Vegas; St. Gertrude the Great, Mora, N.M.
**Mission locations:** Maes, Santiago-Talco, N.M.
Art by Frankie Lucero.

**Santa Ana (1st Century)**
**Feast Day July 26 (feast day combined with St. Joachim—parents of Mary)**
Patroness of housewives, grandmothers and cabinetmakers, Santa Ana was the grandmother of Jesus. She gave birth to Mary, whom she conceived through immaculate conception, at the age of 40. She was married to Joachim, who died right after the birth of Jesus. St. Anne's church in Santa Fe is named in her honor. Patron saint of Santa Ana Pueblo in New Mexico.
**Parish church:** St. John the Baptist, San Juan Pueblo, N.M.
**Mission location:** Alcalde, N.M.
Art by Marie Romero Cash.

**San Ignacio de Loyola (1491–1556)**
**Feast Day July 31**

Patron of the military and of religious retreat; invoked against being overly conscientious. Founder of the Jesuits, San Ignacio was of Basque origin. Although rumor has it that he may have fathered an illegitimate daughter, San Ignacio de Loyola devoted his life to God and the study of the scriptures.

**Parish churches:** Our Lady of Sorrows, Las Vegas; St. Rose of Lima, Santa Rosa, N.M.
**Mission location:** San Ignacio, N.M.
Art by Ramón José López.

**San Juan Diego**
**Feast Day July 31**

Canonized in 2002, Juan Diego was an Aztec native who saw four apparitions of the Virign Mary on Tepeyac Hill in the northern part of Mexico City. During the fourth vision a miraculous image of Our Lady of Guadalupe appeared on Juan Diego's *tilma*.

Art by Archie Perea.

# August

**San Cayetano (1480–1547)**
**Feast Day August 7**

Patron of gamblers, San Cayetano, also known as Gaetano and Cajetán, was one of the great Catholic reformers. Born in Vicenza, Italy, he worked with the sick and the needy and founded an institute of clergy devoted to the reformation of the church.

Art by Arthur López.

**Santo Domingo (1170–1221)**
**Feast Day August 8**

Born in Calaruega, Spain. Patron of astronomers, the Dominican Republic and Santo Domingo Pueblo in New Mexico.
**Parish church:** Holy Family, Chimayó, N.M.
**Mission locaton:** Cundiyó, N.M.
Art by Charles M. Carrillo.

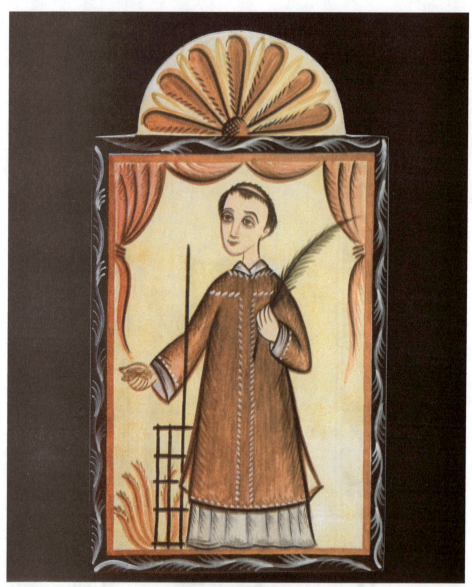

**San Lorenzo (d. 258)**
**Feast Day August 10**

Patron of Ceylon (Sri Lanka), cooks, librarians and the poor; invoked against fire and lumbago. One of the seven deacons of Rome, San Lorenzo was born in Huesca, Spain, and was martyred in Rome. Disobeying an order to collect treasures for the Church, instead he brought the blind, the crippled and other unfortunates to the church leaders and said, "These are the Church's treasures," for which he was burned alive. San Lorenzo is the patron saint of Picurís Pueblo in New Mexico.

**Parish churches:** St. Alice, Mountainair; Our Lady of Sorrows, Bernalillo; Holy Child, Tijeras; San Miguel, Socorro, N.M.

**Mission locations:** Abó, Bernalillo, Cañoncito, Polvadera, N.M.

Art by Arturo Olivas.

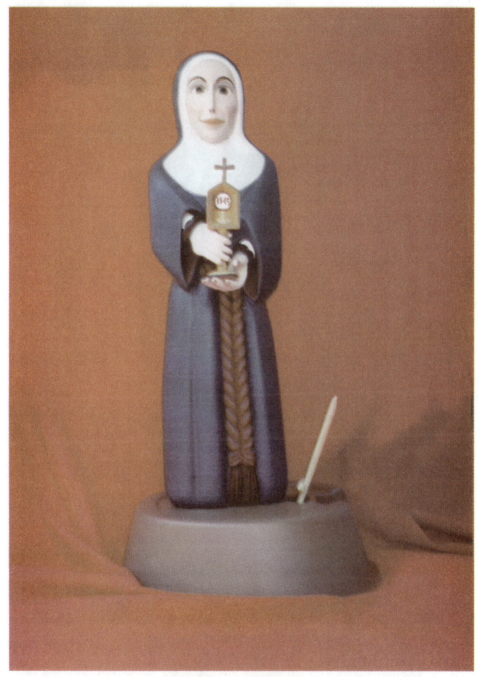

**Santa Clara (1194–1253)**
**Feast Day August 11**

Patroness of embroiderers and employees of the media; invoked against sore eyes. Born in Assisi, Italy, and a follower of St. Francis of Assisi, she founded the contemplative order "Poor Clares." Patron saint of Santa Clara Pueblo in N.M. Art by Archie Perea.

**St. Maximilian Kolbe (1894–1941)**
**Feast Day August 14**

Patron of drug addicts; invoked against drug addiction. Born at Zdunska-Wola, near Lodz, Poland, Fr. Maximilian Kolbe established foundations for the Immaculate Conception near Warsaw and in Japan and India. He was arrested when the Nazis invaded Poland and sent to the Auschwitz concentration camp, where he was killed when he offered to take the place of a married man with children who was scheduled to be executed.

Art by Archie Perea.

**San Roque (1295–1378)**
**Feast Day August 17**

Patron of cattle, doctors, dog lovers and prisoners; invoked against cholera, contagious diseases, skin disease and plague. San Roque was born in Montpellier, France. He devoted himself to caring for victims of the plague that ravaged Italy at the turn of the 14th century. San Roque became sick with the plague himself and was imprisoned as a spy, eventually dying in prison.
Art by Marie A. Luna.

**St. Helen (c. 250–330)**
**Feast Day August 18**

Patroness of archaeologists, St. Helen achieved renown in her 85th year while in the Holy Land where she had a vision in which the location of the long-lost True Cross on which Christ was crucified was revealed to her.

**Parish church:** St. Mary, Vaughn, N.M.

**Mission location:** Pastura, N.M.

Art by Gabriel Vigil.

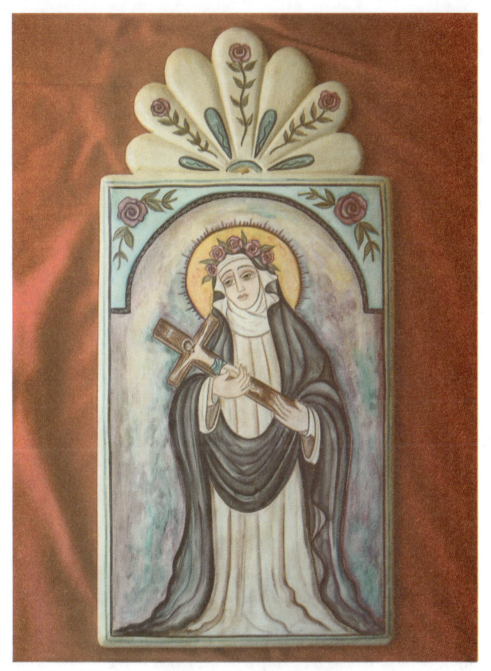

**Santa Rosa de Lima (d. 1586)**
**Feast Day August 23**

Patroness of Central and South America, florists, gardeners, Peru and the Philippines. St. Rose of Lima, Peru, was born in 1586 under the name Isabel de Santa Maria de Flores y del Oliva, fifty years after the Spanish conquest. She was a friend and mentor to San Matín de Porres.

Art by Marie A. Luna.

**San Agustín (354–430)**
**Feast Day August 28**

Patron of brewers and printers, San Agustín was born at Tagaste in northern Africa, where he became the bishop of Hippo. Known as one of the greatest Doctors of the Church, San Agustín molded the thought of Western Christianity. San Agustín is the patron saint of Isleta Pueblo south, of Albuquerque. St. Augustine, Florida, the oldest city in America, was named in his honor by the Spaniards when they arrived there in 1565.

**Parish church:** Our Lady of Sorrow, Las Vegas, N.M.
**Mission location:** San Agustín, N.M.
Art by Carlos Otero.

**San Ramón Nonato (1204–40)**
**Feast Day August 31**

Patron of Catalonia, childbirth, children, midwives, obstetricians and pregnant women; invoked against false accusations. Born in Portella, Catalonia, San Ramón received his name *non natus*, or "not born," when he was delivered by a caesarean operation during which his mother died. San Ramón Nonato was appointed cardinal by Pope Gregory IX in 1239.

Art by Ramón José López.

# September

**Santa Rosalía (d. circa 1160)**
**Feast Day September 4**

Born in Sicily, Santa Rosalía is the principal patroness of Palermo, where she helped to end the plague. She became a hermitess and lived in a cave on Monte Pellegrino near Palermo.

Art by Charles M. Carrillo.

**Santa María Turibia & San Isidro Labrador**
**Feast Day - September 9**

Patrons of all married people and the Holy Couple of Madrid, Spain, San Isidro and Santa María Turibia worked for Juan Diego de Vargas, who led the reconquest of Santa Fe in 1692. San Isidro and Santa María Turibia had a son that died as a baby. The anguished couple, who believed that their son's death was the will of God, dedicated the remainder of their lives to serving the Lord. They agreed to remain celibate for the rest of their lives. Santa María Turibia is also honored as a saint under the name of Santa María de la Cabeza. Her head, which is conserved in a reliquary and carried in procession, has often brought down rain from heaven to replenish the parched countryside.

Art by Arlene Cisneros Sena.

**Triumph of the Holy Cross**
**Feast Day September 14**

Reminds us of the *promesa* made by Diego de Vargas to thank La Conquistadora for safely returning our ancestors from desert exile in the El Paso, Texas area in 1692.

Art by Arlene Cisneros Sena.

**Nuestra Señora de los Dolores**
**Feast Day September 15**

Patroness of troubled mothers.

**Parish churches:** La Santísima Trinidad, Arroyo Seco; Our Lady of Guadalupe, Taos; St. Alice, Mountainair; St. Rose of Lima, Santa Rosa; St. Anthony, Dixon; Our Lady of Guadalupe, Santa Fe; San Francisco de Asís, Ranchos de Taos; San Antonio de Padua, Peñasco; San Juan Nepomuceno, El Rito, N.M.

**Mission churches:** Arroyo Hondo, Cañón, Manzano, Milagro, Pilar, Río en Medio, Telcolote, Vadito, Vallecitos, Willard, N.M.

Art by Arlene Cisneros Sena.

# Otoño

**Padre Pío (1887–1968)**
**Feast Day September 23**

Patron of healing, Padre Pío was born in Pietrelcina in southern Italy. He began as a novitiate with the Capuchín Friars at the age of 15 and was ordained a priest in 1910. On September 20, 1918, the five wounds of our Lord's Passion appeared on his body, making him the first stigmatized priest in the history of the church.
Art by Archie Perea.

**Archangel Michael**
**Feast Day September 29**
Patron of policemen, bankers, grocers, radiologists, paratroopers and the dying; invoked against peril at sea. St. Michael is also a prominent figure in Judaism and Islam.
Art by Jean Anaya Moya.

**Archangels Michael, Gabriel and Raphael**
**Feast Day September 29**
The three angels are liturgically venerated by the church on September 29.
Art by Arlene Cisneros Sena.

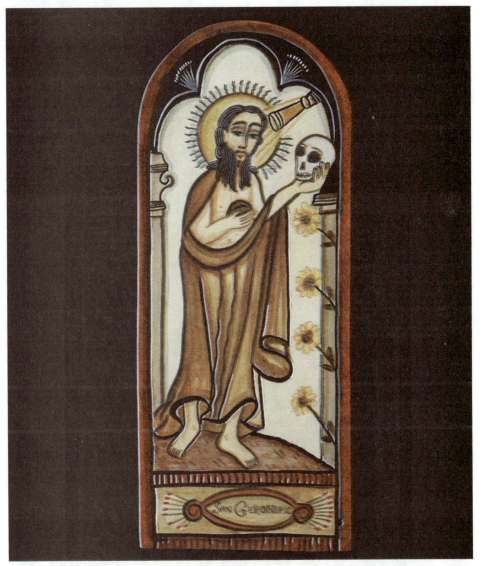

**San Gerónimo (c. 342–420)**
**Feast Day September 30**

Patron of librarians, students and Taos Pueblo, San Gerónimo, who is venerated as a Doctor of the Church, was known as the great translator of the Bible from Greek and Latin. Born at Strido, near Aquileia, Dalmatia (an ancient Roman province which is now western Croatia), San Gerónimo's greatest achievement was his translation of the Old Testament from Hebrew and his revisions of the Latin version of the New Testament in 390–405. This version, called the Vulgate, was declared the official Latin text of the Bible for Catholics, and its English translation was used through the middle of the 20th century.

**Parish church:** Our Lady of Sorrows, Las Vegas, N.M.
**Mission location:** San Gerónimo, N.M.

Art by Nicolás Otero.

# October

**Santa Teresita del Niño Jesús (1873–1897)**
**Feast Day October 1**

Patroness of florists, foreign missions, pilots and France; invoked against tuberculosis. Known as the Little Flower, St. Teresa of Lisieux may one day be declared the third woman Doctor of the Church. A Carmelite nun and follower of Santa Teresa de Ávila, Santa Teresita died of tuberculosis.

**Parish churches:** Nuestra Señora de Guadalupe, Villanueva; Our Lady of Sorrows, Las Vegas; St. Gertrude the Great, Mora, N.M.

**Mission locations:** Gonzales Ranch, St. Thomas the Apostle, Abiquiú, San Agustín, Turquillo, N.M.

Art by Monica Sosaya Halford.

**San Francisco de Asís (1181-1226)**
**Feast Day October 4**

Patron saint of Santa Fe, animals, ecology, Italy, tapestry makers; invoked against fires, for peace and reconciliation in families. Born in Assisi, Italy, to a wealthy family, St. Francis devoted his life to poverty and to concern for the poor and sick. St. Francis is the patron saint of Nambe Pueblo in New Mexico.

**Parish churches:** Sacred Heart of Jesús, Española; St. John the Baptist, San Juan Pueblo; St. Joseph, Cerrillos; Nuestra Señora de Guadalupe, Villanueva, N.M.

**Mission locations:** El Duende, Estaca, Golden, Leyba, N.M.

Art by Gabriel Vigil.

**Nuestra Señora del Rosario,**
**Feast Day October 7**

La Conquistadora, patroness of Santa Fe, maker of miracles, honored with *novenas* and processions throughout New Mexico.
Art by Marie Sena.

Nada Te Turbe - Nada Te Espante
Todo Se Pasa - Con Dios Adelante

**Santa Teresa de Ávila (1515–82)**
**Feast Day October 15**

Patroness of Spain; invoked against headaches and heart disease, first woman Doctor of the Church and reformer of the Carmelites for both women and men. Born in Ávila, Spain, on March 28, she became a Carmelite in 1536. Santa Teresa is known as one of the great mystics of all time; her letters and books continue to be translated into many languages.

Art by Carlos Otero.

**San Lucas (1st Century)**
**Feast Day October 18**

Patron of artists, doctors, butchers, glass workers, goldsmiths, lace makers and notaries and a disciple of St. Paul, San Lucas was the author of the Third Gospel and Acts of the Apostles. He was also a physician and artist who painted several portraits of Mary, who died when he was 84.

Art by Charles M. Carrillo.

**Santa Úrsula**
**Feast Day · October 21**

Patroness of orphans, schoolgirls, tailors, teachers and universities; invoked against plague. According to The Golden Legend, Santa Úrsula was martyred along with 11,000 virgins by the Huns.

Art by Frankie Lucero.

**Rafael the Archangel**
**Feast Day October 24**

Patron of druggists, happy meetings, health inspectors, lovers, travelers and young people leaving home; invoked against blindness. San Rafael, whose name in Hebrew means the one who heals, is identified as the angel who healed the earth. He is venerated in Christianity and Judaism.

**Parish churches:** St. John the Baptist, San Juan Pueblo; St. Gertrude the Great, Mora; Our Lady of Sorrows, Las Vegas, N.M

**Mission locations:** El Guique, La Cueva, Trementina, N.M.

Art by Nicholás Otero.

### St. Jude (1st Century)
### October 28

Patron of the most impossible, hopeless desperate cases, St. Jude is one of the twelve apostles and brother of St. James. Since St. Jude is often associated with Judas, who betrayed Christ, he didn't receive as much attention as the apostles so he had time to take care of the most difficult cases. He was martyred in Persia along with fellow apostle Simon.

Art by Jean Anaya Moya.

# November

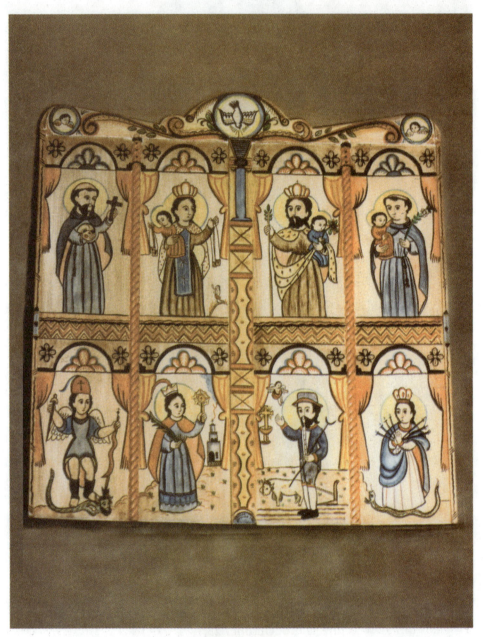

**All Saints Day**
**Feast Day November 1**

All Saints Day is a universal Christian feast that honors and remembers all Christian saints, known and unknown. All Saints is a day to remember, thank God for, but also to venerate and pray to the saints in heaven for assistance.
Art by Charles M. Carrillo.

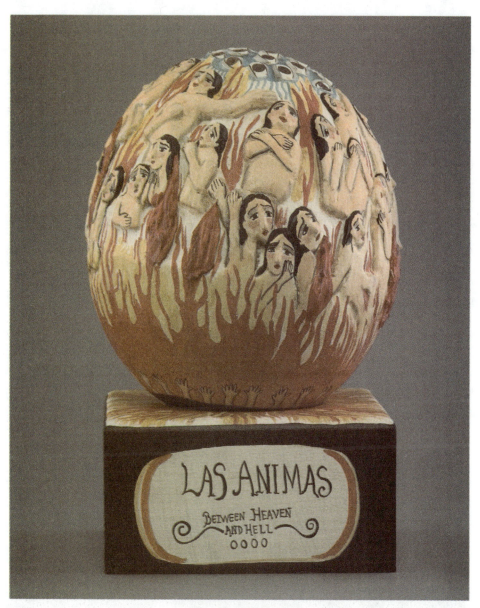

LAS ANIMAS

Between Heaven
and Hell
0000

### All Souls Day
### Feast Day November 2

All Souls Day is the commemoration of the faithful departed in purgatory. Abbot Odilo of Cluny instituted it in the monasteries of his congregation in 998; other religious orders took up the observance, and it was adopted by various dioceses and gradually by the Church as a whole. The Office of the Dead must be recited by the clergy on this day, and Pope Benedict XV granted to all priests the privilege of saying three Masses of requiem: one for the souls in purgatory, one for the intention of the Holy Father, one for the priests. If the feast should fall on a Sunday it is observed on November 3.

Art by Marie Romero Cash.

**San Martín de Porres (1579–1639)**
**Feast Day November 3**

Patron of hairdressers, public health workers, persons of mixed race, racial tensions and Peruvian television, San Martín was born in Lima, Peru, on November 9, the illegitimate son of a Spanish knight and a freed Panamanian. He became a Dominican lay brother in 1594. He founded an orphanage and foundling hospital. He ministered to African slaves brought to Peru and was a close friend and follower of Santa Rosa de Lima. He is reputed to have had supernatural gifts, such as being in two different locations at the same time, and was able to fly.
Art by Marie A. Luna.

**San Andres Avellino (1521–1608)**
**Feast Day November 10**

Born at Castronuovo, Italy, San Andres Avellino was baptized with the name of Lorenzo but changed his name to Andrew when he joined the Theatines in Naples. He spent most of his life there, working to improve the conditions of the clergy and the spiritual needs of the people.

Art by Marie Romero Cash.

**San Diego (c. 1400–63)**
**Feast Day November 13**

Patron of cooks, San Diego was born in San Nicolás del Puerto, Spain. During his youth he lived as a recluse and then became a Franciscan lay brother at Arrizafa. He worked as a missionary in the Canary Islands, becoming the guardian of Fuerteventura there in 1440. Noted for his healing powers and miracles, San Diego died at Alcalá on November 7 and was canonized in 1588. He is the patron of Jemez and Tesuque pueblos in New Mexico.

**Parish church:** Our Lady Of Guadalupe, Santa Fe, N.M.
**Mission location:** Tesuque, N.M.
Art by Charles M. Carrillo.

**Santa Gertrudis (c. 1256–1302)**
**Feast Day November 16**

Known as Gertrude the Great and patroness of the West Indies, Santa Gertrudis was raised by Benedictine nuns at Helfta in Saxony. At the age of 26 she became a nun and had the first of many visions of Christ throughout her lifetime. She became versed in the Bible and the writings of Augustine, Gregory and Bernard and herself became a writer of her supernatural and mystical experiences. Through her writings she helped to spread the devotion of the Sacred Heart.
Art by Rubén Montoya.

**La Fiesta de Cristo Rey**
**Feast Day last Sunday before Advent**

The inspiration of countless martyrs.
**Parish church:** Our Lady of Belén, Belén. N.M.
**Mission location:** Bosque, N.M.
Art by Nicolás Otero.

SANTA CECILIA

### Santa Cecilia
### Feast Day November 22

Patroness of composers, mariachis and all musicians, Santa Cecilia was born in Rome, Italy. She heard angelic harmonies, and could play any instrument and sing any song. Thought to be the inventor of the organ, she was married against her will. At her wedding Santa Cecilia did not hear the nuptial music and sounds of merriment; instead she sat apart, singing to God in her heart.
Art by Monica Sosaya Halford.

**San Andrés (1st Century)**
**Feast Day November 30**

Apostle and patron of fishermen, sailors and spinsters; invoked against gout and neck problems. San Andrés was a fisherman and disciple of both John the Baptist and Jesus Christ. His bones, preserved in Amalfi, Italy, have for fourteen centuries produced a mysterious oil that trickles from his tomb down the aisle of the church on his feast day of November 30 and on January 26 and 28.
Art by Arthur López.

# December

**Santa Bárbara (4th Century)**
**Feast Day December 4**

Patroness of architects, artillery, builders, firefighters, fireworks makers, miners, sailors; invoked against explosions, fire, lightning and sudden death. According to legend, Santa Bárbara lived in a tower where she had three windows built into a bathhouse that her father was constructing to represent the Trinity. Already furious at her for not marrying the Emperor Maximilian, her father, Dioscurus, took her up to a mountain and cut off her head. The beautiful town of Santa Barbara, California, was named for Santa Bárbara by the Spanish mariners who were inspired by her.

**Parish churches:** San Antonio de Padua, Peñasco; Our Lady of Guadalupe, Peña Blanca, N.M.

**Mission locations:** Rodarte, Sile, N.M.

Art by Polly E. Chávez.

### San Nicolás (d. circa 350)
### Feast Day December 6

Patron of bakers, barrel makers, bootblacks, brewers, brides, children, dock workers, fishermen, merchants, pawnbrokers, perfumers, prisoners, sailors, spinsters
and travelers. Also the patron of Greece, San Nicolás was known for his holiness,
zeal and miracles. Born to wealthy parents in Patara, in the western peninsula of
Turkey, San Nicolás devoted himself to the conversion of sinners and gave his
wealth to the poor. Thanks to the Dutch, his legend grew to include the giving of
gifts to children and his name was changed to Santa Claus.
Art by Arthur López.

**Immaculate Conception**
**Feast Day December 8**

Patron of the abandoned pueblo of Quaraí in New Mexico.

**Parish churches:** Immaculate Conception, Tomé; Holy Family, Roy; St. Joseph, Mosquero; Our Lady of Guadalupe, Taos; San Juan Nepomuceno, El Rito, N.M.

**Mission churches:** Casa Colorada, Gallegos, Ranchitos, Tres Piedras, N.M.

Art by Jean Anaya Moya.

**Our Lady of Guadalupe**
**Feast Day December 12**

The first recognized appearances of the Virgin Mary in the Western Hemisphere took place in Mexico City, where legends say she made four visits from December 9 to 12 in 1531 to a native, Juan Diego. She became known as the Virgin Mary of Guadalupe. During her final visit, her image appeared miraculously on the Aztec's cloak (*tilma*). Benedict XIV set the 12th of December as her feast date in 1754: before this date she was celebrated on September 8, the feast of the birth of Mary. Guadalupe is honored globally as the Mother of all People. She is the patron of Zuni Pueblo in New Mexico.

**Parish churches:** San Diego Mission, Jeméz Pueblo; St. Anthony, Questa; St. Xavier, Clayton and St. Anthony of Padua, Pecos; St. Mary, Vaughn; St. Thomas the Apostle, Abiquiú; Sacred Heart of Jesús, Española; St. Gertrude the Great, Mora; Cristo Rey, Santa Fe; San Juan Nepomuceno, El Rito; Our Lady of Belén, Belén; Santa Clara, Wagon Mound; Holy Family, Roy; St. Joseph, Mosquero; St. Anne, Tucumcari; Our Lady of Sorrows, Las Vegas; San José, Antón Chico; St. Anthony, Dixon, N.M.

**Mission locations:** Canyon, Cerro, Des Moines, El Macho, Encino, Gallina, Glorieta, Guachupangue, Guadalupita, La Cañada de Los Alamos, La Madera, Los Chávez, Ocate, Ojo Caliente, Sabinoso, San Jon, Sapello, Tecolotito, Velarde, N.M.

Art by Marie A. Luna.

**Santa Lucía (d. 304)**
**Feast Day December 13**

Patroness of gondoliers, glaziers and lamplighters; invoked against dysentery, eye disease, hemorrhage and throat disease. Born of noble parents in Syracuse, Sicily, Santa Lucía was denounced as a Christian because she refused to marry the suitor chosen by Emperor Diocletian. She was sent to a brothel where she tore her eyes out rather than lose her virginity.
Art by Arthur López.

**San Juan Marinoni**
**Feast Day December 14**

To be beatified later this year, this Theatine saint is responsible for many miraculous cures in San Luis, Colorado.

Art by Marie Romero Cash.

# Invierno

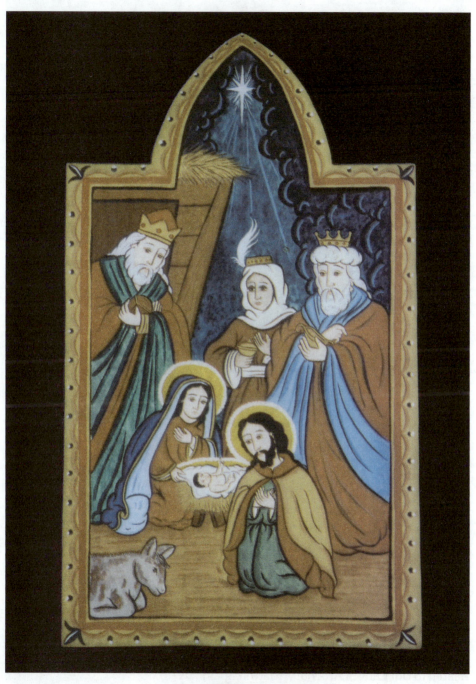

**The Birth of Christ
Feast Day December 2**

Art by Gabriel Vigil.

**Santo Niño de Atocha**
**Feast Day December 25**

Patron of prisoners and soldiers, *Santo Niño de Atocha* was a very popular saint during *World War II* in New Mexico, when familes prayed to him to bring their loved ones home and for an end to the war. *Santo Niño de Atocha* is a very popular devotional figure in Spain, Mexico and New Mexico. Its origin may be related to *Our Lady of Atocha*, in Madrid, Spain.

**Parish churches:** St. Gertrude the Great, Mora; Holy Child, Tijeras, N.M.

**Mission locations:** Buena Vista, Carnuel, N.M.

Art by Ramón José López.

**Holy Family**
**Feast Day December 30**

Devotion to the Holy Family began in earnest in 1892 when economic activity shifted from the home to the factory, undermining the family as an institution. Then in 1994, with the family unit back in crisis, Pope Paul II started a new campaign to promote devotion to the Holy Family.

**Parish churches:** San Miguel, Socorro; Our Lady of Sorrows, Las Vegas, N.M.
**Mission locations:** Lemitar, Variadero, N.M.

Art by Arlene Cisneros Sena.

# About the Artists

Jean Anaya Moya is the daughter of Mary Ann Phillis and José Manuel Anaya. She was born in Santa Fe and raised in the village of Galisteo. Moya began doing devotional art in 1990 and has evolved into an award-winning artist. Her work is in several museums and private collections throughout the world. Photos of artwork by Firefly Studios. The art of Jean Anaya Moya is featured on pages 13, 44, 49, 71, 91, 101 and 113.

Charles M. Carrillo is the son of Loretta Torres and Rafael A. Carrillo. His family has been in New Mexico for hundreds of years. He has been a *santero* since the late 1970s and this past year celebrated his 25th year at Spanish Market. He is an annual award-winner and has received more than 34 ribbons at Spanish Market over the years. His work is exhibited in the collections of major museums, including the Smithsonian Institution in Washington, D.C., the Gene Autry Museum in Los Angeles, the Denver Museum of Art, the International Museum of Folk Art in Santa Fe, the Museum of Spanish Colonial Art in Santa Fe, the National Hispanic Cultural Center in Albuquerque, the Heard Museum in Phoenix and many other institutions and churches. Carrillo is the author of several books, including the most recent, *Saints of the Pueblos*. Photos of Charles M. Carrillo and his artwork by Adrián A. Aragón. The art of Charles M. Carrillo is featured on the inside front cover and pages 6, 52, 77, 86, 98, 102 and 106.

Polly E. Chávez is the daughter of Ramoncita Gurulé and Abrán Sánchez. Her paternal ancestors have been traced to the colonists who came with Juan de Oñate to Nuevo México in 1598. Her Gurulé ancestors have been traced to Frenchman Jacques Grolet, known as "Santiago Gurulé" by fellow colonists who came to Nuevo México in 1693 with Diego de Vargas. Chávez is a *santera* who specializes in *retablos* and has exhibited her work in galleries, libraries and museums throughout New Mexico. She is a frequent speaker on Hispanic arts and crafts, writes a newspaper column for the *Ruidoso News* and is an arts facilitator for Carrizozo Public Schools. The art of Polly E. Chávez is featured on pages 11 and 111.

Arlene Cisneros Sena is the daughter of the late Fred Cisneros and Elsie Martínez Cisneros. Since her entry into Spanish Market in 1992, Sena's work has achieved national and international acclaim. A recipient of numerous awards including the Archbishop of Santa Fe's Award for Excellence, Sena has recently completed a number of prestigious large-scale commissions, among them an altar screen for the Blessed Sacrament Chapel inside Santa Fe's St. Francis Basilica, as well as an altar screen for St. Anne's Church and *retablos* for the churches of Santa María de la Paz and San Ysidro in Tesuque. Photos of Arlene Cisneros Sena and her artwork by Chris Corrie. The art of Arlene Cisneros Sena is featured on the front and back covers and pages 3, 45, 48, 55, 59, 87, 88, 89, 92 and 119.

Horacio Córodva is the son of Epifania Montoya and Anastacio Córdova. He was an educator with 25 years of teaching to the handicapped and to art students. He began his art career first as a potter, then as a sculptor and now he devotes his work to religious art. Because of the prevalence of cancer throughout the country, Córdova paints many San Peregrino *retablos*. His artwork is sold in galleries throughout the country. The art of Horacio Córdova is featured on page 43.

Gustavo Victor Goler is the son of Gustavo Victor Emilio Goler and Ana María Marcomini. He was raised in Santa Fe, New Mexico, among a family of Latin American art conservators and restorers. Goler's early years were spent apprenticing in his family's conservation studios, where he learned wood-carving skills by restoring 18th- and 19-century saints from Latin America. He attended the University of New Mexico and later earned a degree in graphics and advertising from the Colorado Institute of Art. Goler is an award-winning artist whose artwork is featured in museums and churches throughout the country. The art of Gustavo Victor Goler is featured on pages 34, 37 and 51.

Krissa María López-Moya is the daughter of Louise Romero and Felix A. López. She follows in the family tradition of *santeros*; both her father and brother also create *retablos*. She has participated in the Spanish Market for the last fifteen years and her work can be found in churches, museums and private collections throughout the world. The art of Krissa María López-Moya is featured on page 67.

Arthur López is the son of Jerry Rubén López and Cecilia Peña López. He has been working as a *santero* for six years and is represented by Parks Gallery in Taos, New Mexico. López is an award-winning Spanish Market artist. His work can be found in the collections of the Museum of International Folk Art in Santa Fe, NM; the Albuquerque Fine Arts Museum, the Taylor Museum in Colorado Springs, Co., the Denver Art Museum and El Museo Convento in Española, NM and in the Freedom Museum (911 Memorial at Ground Zero), New York City. His work is also featured in numerous private collections throughout the nation. The art of Arthur López is featured on pages 32,56,76,110,112 &115.

Ramón José López is the son of Florentina Archuleta and Lorenzo López. He received a National Endowment for the Arts award in 1997 as well as many local awards throughout his 24-year career as an artist. His work can be found at the Smithsonian Institution in Washington, D.C.; Taylor Fine Arts Musuem in Colorado Springs, Colorado; the Gene Autry Museum in Los Angeles; the International Folk Art Museum in Santa Fe; the Santa Fe Palace of the Governors and private collections throughout the world. López's grandfather, Lorenzo López Sr. was a *santero* and very religious man.

López has followed in his grandfather's footsteps and prays that he is as proud of him as Ramón is of his *abuelo*. The art of Ramón José López is featured on the inside back cover and pages IV, 14, 36, 47, 60, 63, 66, 74, 85 and 118.

Frankie Nasario Lucero, born in 1962, is the son of Nabor and Victoria Lucero and a tenth-generation descendant of Capt. Pedro Lucero de Gudoi, who participated in the Entrada with Juan de Oñate. Lucero is an award-winning *santero* (*bultos, retablos* and reliefs) whose work is featured in museums and private collections throughout the world. The art of Frankie Nasario Lucero is featured on pages 38, 53, 57, 65, 72 and 99.

Marie A. Luna is the daughter of Jack P. Trujillo and Margaret De La O Luján. Luna has participated in the summer and winter Spanish Markets since 2003, which she considers a blessing because of the opportunity it provides to meet so many wonderful and talented people. She believes good energy must go into creating every *retablo* because each one has its destination. In the process of painting her *retablos* she uses homemade gesso, natural pigments, piñón varnish and beeswax. The art of Marie A. Luna is featured on pages 81, 83, 104 and 114.

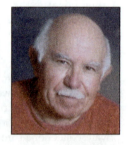

Richard Montoya is the son of Donelia Esquivel and Daniel Montoya, Sr. His artwork is at the Smithsonian Institution, as well as museums and churches around the world. He has taught the art of *retablo* painting through the CEED program for several years. The art of Richard Montoya is featured on page 62.

Rubén O. Montoya is the son of Dolores Ortiz Kozlowski and is a World War II Purple Heart and Bronze Medal recipient. He retired from Los Alamos National Laboratory in 1973 and since then has devoted his life to religious art. His work is featured in museums in Berlin, Moscow, Oklahoma, Missouri, Arkansas and South Carolina. The art of Rubén Montoya is featured on pages 2 and 107.

Arturo Olivas is the son of José Natividad Olivas and Elisa Alva. Olivas has been an exhibitor in the Spanish Market for ten years and is the recipient of many awards for his artwork. His work can be found in many museums, including: the Southwest Musuem, the Gene Autry Museum, the California Craft and Folk Art Museum, the Mexican Museum in San Francisco, the Eiteljorg Museum, the Museum of International Folk Art, the Heard Museum, the Denver Art Musuem and the Copia Museum. His art can also be found in many private and public collections, including the Regis Collection and the Spanish Embassy in Madrid, Spain. The art of Arturo Olivas is featured on pages 39, 70 and 78.

Carlos José Otero is the son of Oralia Chávez de Otero and Ramón Otero. He is a poet, historian and *santero* from Los Lunas and Tomé, New Mexico. Otero has been an award-winning Spanish Market artist since 1996. He won first place at the 2005 New Mexico State Fair for his work *La Reina de Paz*. The art of Carlos José Otero is featured on pages 1, 5, 42, 58, 84 and 97.

Nicolás Roldón Otero is the son of Jeanette Madrid Otero and Steven Roldón Otero from El Cerro, New Mexico. His work may be found in several museums and private collections. Otero has received a first-place award in Santa Fe's Spanish Market. Born in 1981, he has been featured in many publications and has received national and local attention. An avid student of Spanish Colonial art, Otero teaches and lectures on the subject. His work is shown in many galleries and juried exhibitions. He is currently finishing his degree in art education at the University of New Mexico. The art of Nicolás Roldón Otero is featured on pages VI, X, 7, 8, 31, 64, 93, 100 and 108.

Henry Parra is the son of Joaquín Galindo Parra and Guillermina López. He was born in Los Angles to a New Mexican family that, as colonists, long ago lived beside the Río Grande in New Mexico, later to migrate as early settlers of Grant County and the secluded Mimbres Valley. A former northern New Mexico administrator, Parra has most recently been an educator in secondary education and with the regional universities. Saint-making became Parra's healing therapy long ago, following serious illness and open-heart surgery. Parra and his family are included in the book *Remnants of Crypto-Jews Among Hispanic Americans*. The art of Henry Parra is featured on pages 4, 12 and 50.

Archie Perea is the son of Luis Perea and Adela Felix and is a lifelong resident of La Ciénega. His father was a carver and a carpenter, which inspired Perea to learn his craft. A *santero* since 1972, he enjoys carving saints and animals. He's very grateful to the numerous people who continue to collect his artwork. The art of Archie Perea is featured on pages 75, 79, 80 and 90.

Marie Romero Cash is the daughter of the late Emilio and Senaida Romero, traditional tinsmiths whose innovative works earned them numerous awards during their lifetimes. She has created Stations of the Cross for the Basilica of St. Francis in Santa Fe, St. John's Methodist Church in Albuquerque, and churches in San Luis and Pueblo, Colorado. She has received many awards at Spanish Market, where she has participated for thirty years, including the Master's Award for Lifetime Achievement. She has been honored by the National Endowment for the Arts, the New Mexico Endowment for the Humanities, and Women in the Arts. Cash has had several one-person shows at prestigious galleries and museums throughout the Southwest. Her works grace many museum and private collections as well. An avid writer and historian, she has published several books about northern New Mexican *santos*, churches, and women's shrines. The art of Marie Romero Cash is featured on page I, 17-30, 73, 103, 105 and 116.

Carlos Santistevan is the son of Barbara Olivas and Rodolfo Santistevan. He is an award-winning *santero* whose work is featured in the National Museum of American Art in Washington, D.C., the International Folk Art Museum in Santa Fe, The Millicent Rogers Museum in Taos and the Regis University Collection in Denver. The art of Carlos Santistevan is featured on pages 9 and 10.

Marie Sena is the daughter of Philip Sena and Laura Hirschboeck. She became a *santera* nine years ago and is proud to be involved in preserving and innovating this tradition. Currently, she is attending graduate school at the University of Texas at Southwestern Medical Center in Dallas and will receive a degree in medical illustration. The art of Marie Sena is featured on 15, 16, 40, 46, 54 and 96.

Monica Sosaya Halford is the daughter of Victoria Sosaya and Agustín Sosaya, whose ancestors came to New Mexico in 1598. She has been interested in art since childhood and has been part of the Spanish Market since 1979. Among the many honors she's received are the Master Achievement Award, the Santa Fe Mayor's Award and the Governor's Award. Several museums, churches and private collectors include her work in their collections of *santos*. The art of Monica Sosaya Halford is featured on pages 41, 61, 68, 69, 94 and 109.

Gabriel Vigil is the son of Elizabeth Chávez and Raymond Sedillo. He has been an award-winning artist with the Santa Fe Spanish Market for the past twelve years. His depiction of the Stations of the Cross can be found at St. Thomas Aquinas church in Phoenix, Arizona. His artwork is in private collections around the country, including a *retablo* that was presented to President Bill and Hillary Clinton that is now part of the Smithsonian collection. The art of Gabriel Vigil is featured on pages XII, 33, 35, 82, 95 and 117.